ATTAINMENT'S
Daily WRITING JOURNAL

Pamela J. Mims • Angel Lee • Tracie-Lynn Zakas • Diane M. Browder

Daily Writing Journal

Pamela J. Mims
Angel Lee
Tracie-Lynn Zakas
Diane M. Browder

Graphic design: Elizabeth Ragsdale & Heidi Barnhill
Editing: Linda R. Schreiber

An Attainment Company Publication
©2013 Attainment Company, Inc. All rights reserved.
Printed in the United States of America
ISBN: 1-57861-844-4

P.O. Box 930160 • Verona, Wisconsin 53593-0160 USA
Phone: 800-327-4269 • Fax: 800.942.3865
www.AttainmentCompany.com

Contents

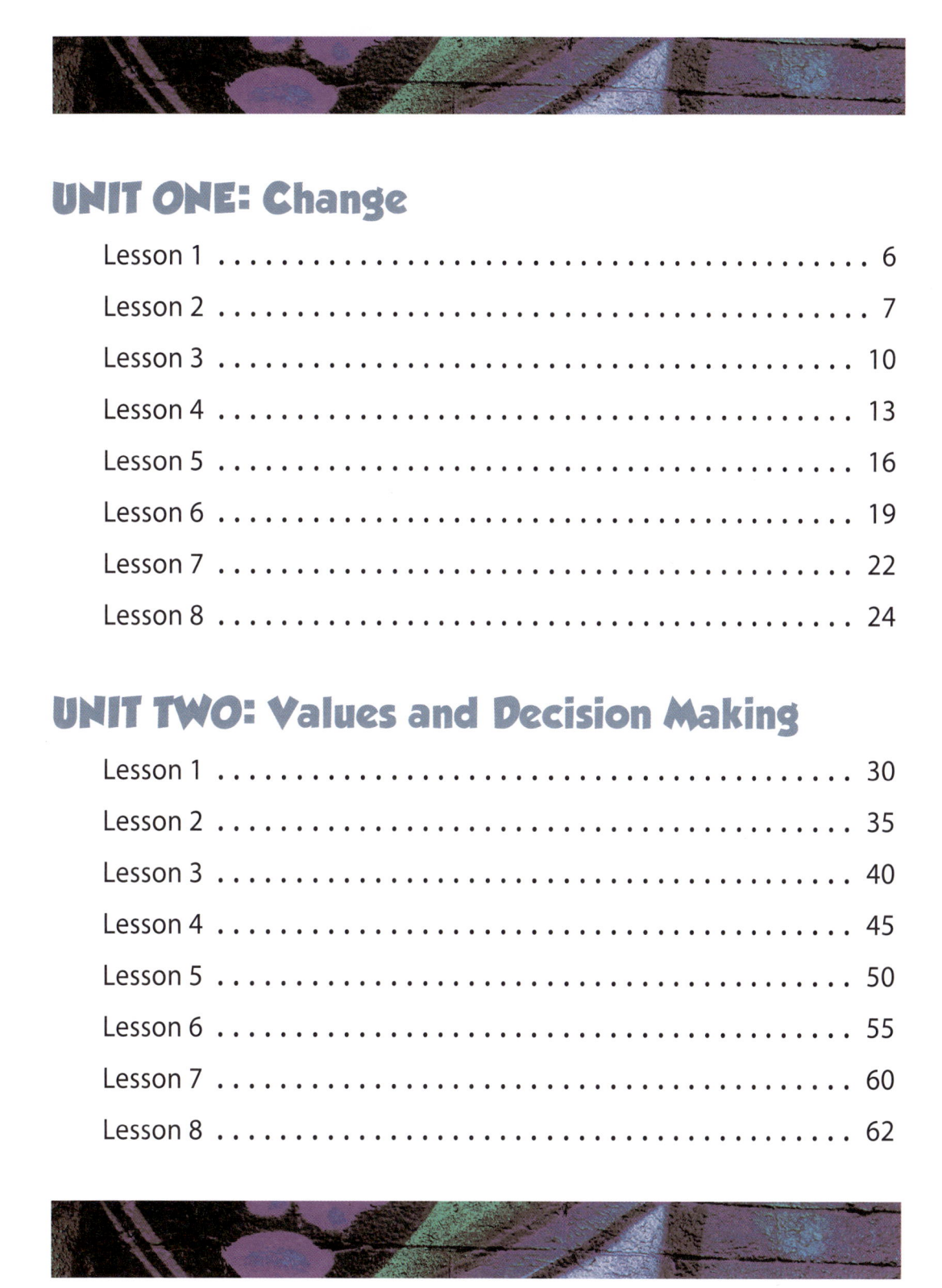

UNIT ONE: Change

Lesson 1 6
Lesson 2 7
Lesson 3 10
Lesson 4 13
Lesson 5 16
Lesson 6 19
Lesson 7 22
Lesson 8 24

UNIT TWO: Values and Decision Making

Lesson 1 30
Lesson 2 35
Lesson 3 40
Lesson 4 45
Lesson 5 50
Lesson 6 55
Lesson 7 60
Lesson 8 62

UNIT THREE: Social Justice

- Lesson 1 68
- Lesson 2 74
- Lesson 3 80
- Lesson 4 86
- Lesson 5 92
- Lesson 6 98
- Lesson 7 102
- Lesson 8 103

UNIT FOUR: Global Awareness

- Lesson 1 106
- Lesson 2 111
- Lesson 3 116
- Lesson 4 121
- Lesson 5 128
- Lesson 6 136
- Lesson 7 140
- Lesson 8 143

LESSON 1  Give your opinion

Who do you like best in the story?

I like _____

_____

_____

_____.

1 Stanley

2 the judge

3 great-great grandfather

LESSON 2 — Give your opinion

Do you think Stanley liked to dig holes?

I think _____

_____

_____

_____ .

1 yes, Stanley liked to dig holes

2 no, Stanley did not like to dig holes

LESSON 2 — Give your opinion

Do you think Camp Green Lake was fun?

I think _____

_____

_____

_____ .

1 yes, Camp Green Lake was fun

2 no, Camp Green Lake was not fun

LESSON 2  # Support your opinion

Support your opinion with a fact from the story.

I think Camp Green Lake   **was / was not**   fun because

_____

_____

_____.

1 Stanley could swim all day

2 Stanley could meet friends

3 Stanley had to dig holes all day

LESSON 3 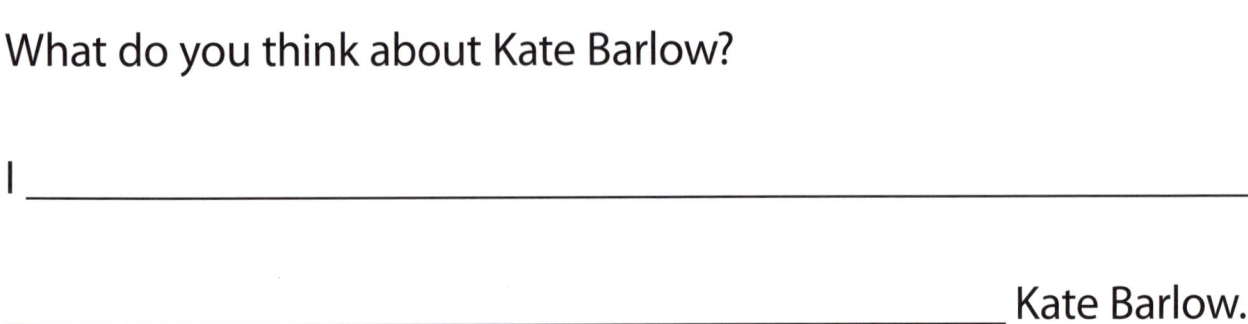 Give your opinion

What do you think about Kate Barlow?

I _____

_____ Kate Barlow.

1 liked

2 did not like

LESSON 3

Give your opinion

What do you think about Trout Walker?

He was a _____

_____.

1 good man

2 bad man

LESSON 3

Support your opinion

Support your opinion with a fact from the story.

I think Trout Walker was a **good / bad** man because _____

_____

_____

_____.

1 he was rich

2 he killed Sam

3 he got mad at Kate

4 he had a fast boat

LESSON 4

Give your opinion

Who was lucky?

_____ was a lucky boy

to have a friend like Stanley.

1 The lizard

2 Zero

3 The girl

4 Mr. Sir

LESSON 4

Give your opinion

What do you think about Mr. Sir?

Mr. Sir was a _____

_____.

1 good man

2 bad man

LESSON 4 — **Support your opinion**

Support your opinion with a fact from the story.

I think Mr. Sir was a   **good / bad**   man because _____

_____

_____

_____ .

1 he dumped Stanley's canteen of water

2 he was a cowboy

3 he had a hat

4 he did not fill Stanley's canteen with water

LESSON 5 — **Give your opinion**

How do you feel about Zero stealing the sneakers?

It was _____ that Zero stole the sneakers.

1 good

2 bad

LESSON 5

Give your opinion

How do you think Stanley and Zero felt about eating onions?

I think Stanley and Zero felt _____

they had onions to eat.

1 glad

2 sad

DAILY WRITING JOURNAL • Unit One • 17

LESSON 5  Support your opinion

Support your opinion with a fact from the story.

I think Stanley and Zero felt **glad** / **sad** because _____

_____

_____

_____.

1 they got sick

2 onions saved them from the lizards

3 they were very hungry

4 they smelled bad

LESSON 6 — Give your opinion

How do you feel about having friends?

Having friends is _____.

1 helpful

2 not helpful

LESSON 6 — Give your opinion

How would you like living in the projects?

I _____ like living in the projects.

1 would

2 would not

LESSON 6

Support your opinion

Support your opinion with a fact from the story.

I think I **would / would not** like living in the projects

because _____

_____

_____.

1 I would have a lot of friends

2 I could play in the park

3 I might get hurt

4 it could be dangerous

DAILY WRITING JOURNAL • Unit One • 21

LESSON 7

Give your opinion

What do you think Maya Angelou meant when she wrote: "You may shoot me with your words"?

I think she was talking about someone _____

_____.

1 yelling

2 smiling

3 with guns

22 • DAILY WRITING JOURNAL • Unit One

LESSON 7 — Give your opinion

I think "shooting someone with words" is a _____

_____ way to talk to others.

1 good

2 bad

LESSON 8

KWHL: Know

What do you know after reading **Changes?**

After reading **Changes,** I know _____

_____

_____ .

1 a butterfly is an insect

2 there is a box on the floor

3 the egg is fixed to the leaf

LESSON 8 — KWHL: Want

After reading **Changes,** what else do you want to know?

I want to know _____

_____

_____.

1 what butterflies eat

2 how to milk a cow

3 how long butterflies live

LESSON 8   **KWHL: How**

How can you find the answers to what you want to know?

I can research my topic by using _____

_____

_____.

1 a book about butterflies

2 an encyclopedia

3 the Internet

LESSON 8

KWHL: Learn

After doing research, what did you learn?

I learned that _____

_____

_____.

1 butterflies eat up to 5 times their body weight in a day

2 butterflies eat leaves

3 butterflies can be many colors

LESSON 8 Select a new topic

Another topic I would like to know more about is _____

_____

_____ .

1 whales

2 manatees

3 cats

4 dogs

LESSON 1   **Give your opinion**

Johnny and Ponyboy met two girls at the drive-in. What did you think of the girls?

The girls at the drive-in were _____.

1 nice

2 trouble

30 • DAILY WRITING JOURNAL • Unit Two

LESSON 1  # Support your opinion

Support your opinion with a fact from the story.

I think the girls were   **nice / trouble**   because _____

_____

_____

_____.

1 they asked the boys to sit with them

2 they went to get soda

3 they talked during the movie

4 they were in a group called the Socs

DAILY WRITING JOURNAL • Unit Two

LESSON 1

Critique your opinion

Do you still feel the same way, or have you changed your opinion? If you feel the same way, add another fact here to support your opinion. If you changed your mind, go to the next page.

☐ I have the same opinion.

I think the girls were **nice / trouble** because _____

_____

_____

and _____

_____.

1 they asked the boys to sit with them

2 they went to get soda

3 they talked during the movie

4 they were in a group called the Socs

LESSON 1  **Critique your opinion** (continued)

If you changed your mind, write a new opinion and support it with two facts.

☐ I changed my opinion.

Now I think the girls were   **nice / trouble**   because _____

_____

_____

and _____

_____.

1 they asked the boys to sit with them

2 they went to get soda

3 they talked during the movie

4 they were in a group called the Socs

DAILY WRITING JOURNAL • Unit Two • 33

LESSON 1 — Give your opinion

What is your opinion about _____?

I think _____

_____

_____

_____

_____ .

LESSON 2

Give your opinion

Johnny and Ponyboy went to the empty lot. Was that a good idea or a bad idea?

I think this was a _____.

1 good idea

2 bad idea

LESSON 2  Support your opinion

Support your opinion with a fact from the story.

I think it was a **good / bad** idea that Johnny and Ponyboy went to the empty lot because _____

_____

_____.

1 they went there to calm down

2 Johnny ended up killing a Soc

3 the Socs tried to drown Ponyboy

4 Johnny and Ponyboy could hang out together there

LESSON 2

Critique your opinion

Do you still feel the same way, or have you changed your opinion? If you feel the same way, add another fact here to support your opinion. If you changed your mind, go to the next page.

☐ I have the same opinion.

I think it was a   **good / bad**   idea that Johnny and Ponyboy

went to the empty lot because _____

_____

and _____

_____.

1 they went there to calm down

2 Johnny ended up killing a Soc

3 the Socs tried to drown Ponyboy

4 Johnny and Ponyboy could hang out together there

DAILY WRITING JOURNAL • Unit Two • 37

LESSON 2

Critique your opinion (continued)

If you changed your mind, write a new opinion and support it with two facts.

☐ I changed my opinion.

Now I think it was a **good / bad** idea that Johnny and

Ponyboy went to the empty lot because _____

_____

and _____

_____.

1 they went there to calm down

2 Johnny ended up killing a Soc

3 the Socs tried to drown Ponyboy

4 Johnny and Ponyboy could hang out together there

LESSON 2

Give your opinion

What is your opinion about _____?

I think _____

_____

_____

_____

_____ .

LESSON 3

Give your opinion

Johnny saw the church burning and went in to save the kids. Was that a good choice or a bad choice?

I think Johnny going into the burning church to save the kids

was a _____.

1 good choice

2 bad choice

LESSON 3

Support your opinion

Support your opinion with a fact from the story.

I think it was a **good choice** / **bad choice** for Johnny to go

into the burning church to save the kids because _____

_____

_____.

1 he got the kids out safely

2 he got hurt

3 he could have gotten trapped

4 kids were trapped inside

LESSON 3

Critique your opinion

Do you still feel the same way, or have you changed your opinion? If you feel the same way, add another fact here to support your opinion. If you changed your mind, go to the next page.

☐ I have the same opinion.

I think it was a **good choice** / **bad choice** for Johnny to go

into the burning church to save the kids because _____

_____

and _____

_____.

1 he got the kids out safely

2 he got hurt

3 he could have gotten trapped

4 kids were trapped inside

LESSON 3   **Critique your opinion** (continued)

If you changed your mind, write a new opinion and support it with two facts.

☐ I changed my opinion.

Now I think it was a **good choice / bad choice** for Johnny to

go into the burning church to save the kids because _____

_____

and _____

_____.

1 he got the kids out safely

2 he got hurt

3 he could have gotten trapped

4 kids were trapped inside

LESSON 3   **Give your opinion**

What is your opinion about _____?

I think _____

_____

_____

_____

_____.

LESSON 4

Give your opinion

Ponyboy chose to fight in the rumble. Was that okay?

I think it was _____ for Ponyboy

to fight in the rumble.

1 okay

2 not okay

LESSON 4

Support your opinion

Support your opinion with a fact from the story.

I think it was **okay / not okay** for Ponyboy to fight in the rumble because _____

_____

_____.

1 the whole gang was going to fight

2 someone could get hurt badly

3 Greasers stick together

4 he knew it was wrong to fight

LESSON 4 — Critique your opinion

Do you still feel the same way, or have you changed your opinion? If you feel the same way, add another fact here to support your opinion. If you changed your mind, go to the next page.

☐ I have the same opinion.

I think it was **okay / not okay** for Ponyboy to fight in the

rumble because _____

_____

and _____

_____.

1 the whole gang was going to fight

2 someone could get hurt badly

3 Greasers stick together

4 he knew it was wrong to fight

DAILY WRITING JOURNAL • Unit Two

LESSON 4   **Critique your opinion** (continued)

If you changed your mind, write a new opinion and support it with two facts.

☐ I changed my opinion.

Now I think it was **okay / not okay** for Ponyboy to fight in

the rumble because _____

_____

and _____

_____.

1 the whole gang was going to fight

2 someone could get hurt badly

3 Greasers stick together

4 he knew it was wrong to fight

LESSON 4

Give your opinion

What is your opinion about _____?

I think _____

_____

_____

_____

_____.

LESSON 5 — **Give your opinion**

How do you think the brothers felt about each other?

I think the brothers _____

_____ each other.

1 loved

2 did not love

LESSON 5

Support your opinion

Support your opinion with a fact from the story.

I think the brothers   **loved / did not love**   each other

because _____

_____

_____.

1 Soda ran out the door to get away from his brother

2 they only had each other

3 they fought and yelled at each other

4 the brothers took time to talk together

LESSON 5

Critique your opinion

Do you still feel the same way, or have you changed your opinion? If you feel the same way, add another fact here to support your opinion. If you changed your mind, go to the next page.

☐ I have the same opinion.

I think that the brothers **loved / did not love** each other

because _____

_____

and _____

_____.

1 Soda ran out the door to get away from his brother

2 they only had each other

3 they fought and yelled at each other

4 the brothers took time to talk together

LESSON 5 — **Critique your opinion** (continued)

If you changed your mind, write a new opinion and support it with two facts.

☐ I changed my opinion.

Now I think that the brothers **loved / did not love** each other because _____

_____

and _____

_____.

1 Soda ran out the door to get away from his brother

2 they only had each other

3 they fought and yelled at each other

4 the brothers took time to talk together

DAILY WRITING JOURNAL • Unit Two

LESSON 5 — # Give your opinion

What is your opinion about _____?

I think _____

_____

_____

_____

_____.

LESSON 6

Give your opinion

In the story, Japanese-American citizens were sent to camps. Was that a good idea or a bad idea?

I think it was a _____

idea to send Japanese-Americans to the camps.

1 good

2 bad

DAILY WRITING JOURNAL • Unit Two • 55

LESSON 6 — Support your opinion

Support your opinion with a fact from the story.

I think it was a **good / bad** idea to send Japanese-Americans to the camps because _____

_____

_____.

1 Japan bombed Hawaii

2 they were not from the United States

3 they could not leave the camps

4 it was not fair to them

LESSON 6

Critique your opinion

Do you still feel the same way, or have you changed your opinion? If you feel the same way, add another fact here to support your opinion. If you changed your opinion, go to the next page.

☐ I have the same opinion.

I think it was a **good** / **bad** idea to send all Japanese-Americans to the camps because _____

_____

and _____

_____.

1 Japan bombed Hawaii

2 they were not from the United States

3 they could not leave the camps

4 it was not fair to them

LESSON 6 **Critique your opinion** (continued)

If you changed your mind, write a new opinion and support it with two facts.

☐ I changed my opinion.

Now I think it was a **good / bad** idea to send Japanese-Americans to the camps because _____

_____

and _____

_____.

1 Japan bombed Hawaii

2 they were not from the United States

3 they could not leave the camps

4 it was not fair to them

LESSON 6

Give your opinion

What is your opinion about _____?

I think _____

_____

_____

_____

_____ .

DAILY WRITING JOURNAL • Unit Two

LESSON 7 — **Give your opinion**

What do you think the poet's intent or meaning of the poem was?

I think the poet was talking about someone being _____

_____.

1 happy

2 sleepy

3 hopeful

LESSON 7 — Give your opinion

Is it good or bad to follow your dreams?

I think it is _____ to follow your dreams.

1 good

2 bad

LESSON 8

KWHL: Know

After reading **Gandhi,** what do you know?

From the passage about Gandhi, I know _____

_____

_____.

1 Gandhi was from India

2 Gandhi drove a car

3 civil rights give everyone the same rights and privileges

LESSON 8 — KWHL: Want

Is there anything else about Gandhi you want to know?

I want to know about _____

_____

_____.

1 the special robes he wore

2 his family

3 his childhood

DAILY WRITING JOURNAL • Unit Two

LESSON 8

KWHL: How

How can you find the answers to what you want to know?

I can research my topic by using _____

_____

_____.

1 a book about Gandhi

2 an encyclopedia

3 a blank piece of paper

4 the Internet

LESSON 8

KWHL: Learn

After doing research, what did you learn?

I learned that _____

_____

_____.

1 Gandhi made his robe from special cloth

2 Gandhi washed windows

3 Gandhi was from India and did not believe in violence

LESSON 8   KWHL

Fill in the KWHL chart.

Research Topic _____

KWHL Chart

What do you Know?	
What do you Want to know?	
How can you find out?	
What did you Learn?	

UNIT THREE
Social Justice

LESSON 1 — **Give your opinion**

The girls were running home from school. What is your opinion about them running home from school?

I think it was _____

_____ that the girls ran home.

1 good

2 dangerous

LESSON 1 — **Support your opinion**

Support your opinion with a fact from the story.

I think it was   **good / dangerous**   that the girls ran home

because _____

_____

_____.

1 they got stopped by the soldiers

2 their families were waiting for them

3 it made them look like hoodlums

4 they got to practice for the race on Friday at school

LESSON 1

Critique your opinion

Do you still feel the same way, or have you changed your opinion? If you feel the same way, add another fact here to support your opinion. If you changed your mind, go to the next page.

☐ I have the same opinion.

I think it was   **good / dangerous**   that the girls ran home

because _____

_____

and _____

_____ .

1 they got stopped by the soldiers

2 their families were waiting for them

3 it made them look like hoodlums

4 they got to practice for the race on Friday at school

70 • DAILY WRITING JOURNAL • Unit Three

LESSON 1   **Critique your opinion** (continued)

If you changed your mind, write a new opinion and support it with two facts.

☐ I changed my opinion.

Now I think it was **good / dangerous** that the girls ran home because _____

_____

and _____

_____.

1 they got stopped by the soldiers

2 their families were waiting for them

3 it made them look like hoodlums

4 they got to practice for the race on Friday at school

DAILY WRITING JOURNAL • Unit Three

LESSON 1

Argue your opinion

Complete the chart below.

My opinion is . . .
_____   _____

I believe this because . . .
_____   _____

Another reason I think this is because . . .
_____   _____

You are now ready to argue your opinion!

LESSON 1

Give your opinion

What do you think about _____?

Write your opinion.

_____

_____

_____

_____

_____ .

LESSON 2 — **Give your opinion**

What do you think it was like to live in Copenhagen during the war?

I think it was _____

_____ to live in Copenhagen during the war.

1 fun

2 scary

LESSON 2 — **Support your opinion**

Support your opinion with a fact from the story.

I think it was **fun / scary** to live in Copenhagen during the war because _____

_____

_____ .

1 Jews had to hide from the Nazis

2 the girls got to play with paper dolls

3 the girls got to see a real king

4 soldiers would search your house

LESSON 2 — **Critique your opinion**

Do you still feel the same way, or have you changed your opinion? If you feel the same way, add another fact here to support your opinion. If you changed your mind, go to the next page.

☐ I have the same opinion.

I think it was **fun / scary** to live in Copenhagen during the war because _____

_____

and _____

_____.

1 Jews had to hide from the Nazis

2 the girls got to play with paper dolls

3 the girls got to see a real king

4 soldiers would search your house

LESSON 2 — **Critique your opinion** (continued)

If you changed your mind, write a new opinion and support it with two facts.

☐ I changed my opinion.

Now I think it was **fun / scary** to live in Copenhagen during

the war because _____

_____

and _____

_____.

1 Jews had to hide from the Nazis

2 the girls got to play with paper dolls

3 the girls got to see a real king

4 soldiers would search your house

DAILY WRITING JOURNAL • Unit Three • 77

LESSON 2 — # Argue your opinion

Complete the chart below.

My opinion is . . .
 _____ _____
I believe this because . . .
 _____ _____
Another reason I think this is because . . .
 _____ _____

You are now ready to argue your opinion!

LESSON 2

Give your opinion

What do you think about _____?

Write your opinion.

_____

_____

_____

_____

_____.

LESSON 3 **Give your opinion**

Number the Stars talks about brave people. Who do you think was brave in this story?

I think _____

_____ was brave.

1 Annemarie

2 Uncle Henrik

LESSON 3

Support your opinion

Support your opinion with a fact from the story.

I think **Annemarie** / **Uncle Henrik** was brave because _____

_____

_____

_____.

1 he helped Jewish people be safe

2 she kept a secret from the soldiers

3 he took the Rosens to Sweden in his boat

4 she was helping the Rosens stay safe

LESSON 3

Critique your opinion

Do you still feel the same way, or have you changed your opinion? If you feel the same way, add another fact here to support your opinion. If you changed your mind, go to the next page.

☐ I have the same opinion.

I think   **Annemarie / Uncle Henrik**   was brave because _____

_____

_____

and _____

_____.

1 he helped Jewish people be safe

2 she kept a secret from the soldiers

3 he took the Rosens to Sweden in his boat

4 she was helping the Rosens stay safe

LESSON 3

Critique your opinion (continued)

If you changed your mind, write a new opinion and support it with two facts.

☐ I changed my opinion.

Now I think   **Annemarie / Uncle Henrik**   was brave because

_____

_____

and _____

_____.

1 he helped Jewish people be safe

2 she kept a secret from the soldiers

3 he took the Rosens to Sweden in his boat

4 she was helping the Rosens stay safe

LESSON 3

Argue your opinion

Complete the chart below.

My opinion is . . .
_____
_____
I believe this because . . .
_____
_____
Another reason I think this is because . . .
_____
_____

You are now ready to argue your opinion!

LESSON 3 — **Give your opinion**

What do you think about _____?

Write your own opinion.

_____

_____

_____

_____

_____.

LESSON 4 **Give your opinion**

How did this part of the story make you feel?

This part of the story made me feel _____

_____ .

1 happy

2 scared

3 proud

4 sad

LESSON 4 — **Give your opinion**

How did you like this part of the story?

I _____

_____ Chapters 7 and 8.

1 liked

2 did not like

LESSON 4 — Support your opinion

Support your opinion with a fact from the story.

I **liked** / **did not like** Chapters 7 and 8 because _____

_____

_____

_____.

1 Annemarie had courage to take the package to Uncle Henrik

2 Annemarie was running down a path when it was cold and dark

3 Annemarie was brave when the soldiers stopped her

4 Annemarie cried because Ellen had to leave

88 • DAILY WRITING JOURNAL • Unit Three

LESSON 4

Critique your opinion

Do you still feel the same way, or have you changed your opinion? If you feel the same way, add another fact here to support your opinion. If you changed your opinion, go to the next page.

☐ I have the same opinion.

I **liked / did not like** Chapters 7 and 8 because _____

_____

_____

and _____

_____.

1 Annemarie had courage to take the package to Uncle Henrik

2 Annemarie was running down a path when it was cold and dark

3 Annemarie was brave when the soldiers stopped her

4 Annemarie cried because Ellen had to leave

DAILY WRITING JOURNAL • Unit Three • **89**

LESSON 4

Critique your opinion (continued)

If you changed your mind, write a new opinion and support it with two facts.

☐ I changed my opinion.

Now I think I **liked / did not like** Chapters 7 and 8 because

_____

_____

and _____

_____.

1 Annemarie had courage to take the package to Uncle Henrik

2 Annemarie was running down a path when it was cold and dark

3 Annemarie was brave when the soldiers stopped her

4 Annemarie cried because Ellen had to leave

LESSON 4

Argue your opinion

Complete the chart below.

My opinion is . . .

I believe this because . . .

Another reason I think this is because . . .

You are now ready to argue your opinion!

LESSON 5 — **Give your opinion**

This unit is about social justice. Was the story a good example of social justice?

The book **Number the Stars** was a _____

_____ example of social justice.

1 good

2 bad

LESSON 5

Support your opinion

Support your opinion with a fact from the story.

I think the book was a   **good / bad**   example of social justice

because _____

_____

_____ .

1 people like the Johansens and Peter helped the Rosens escape

2 the Nazi soldiers took all the sugar and butter

3 Uncle Henrik took Jewish people in his boat to be safe in Sweden

4 the Rosens had to leave their homes or worry about being killed

LESSON 5 — **Critique your opinion**

Do you still feel the same way, or have you changed your opinion? If you feel the same way, add another fact here to support your opinion. If you changed your mind, go to the next page.

☐ I have the same opinion.

I think the book was a **good / bad** example of social justice

because _____

_____

and _____

_____.

1 people like the Johansens and Peter helped the Rosens escape

2 the Nazi soldiers took all the sugar and butter

3 Uncle Henrik took Jewish people in his boat to be safe in Sweden

4 the Rosens had to leave their homes or worry about being killed

LESSON 5

Critique your opinion (continued)

If you changed your mind, write a new opinion and support it with two facts.

☐ I changed my opinion.

Now I think the book was a **good / bad** example of social justice because _____

_____

and _____

_____.

1 people like the Johansens and Peter helped the Rosens escape

2 the Nazi soldiers took all the sugar and butter

3 Uncle Henrik took Jewish people in his boat to be safe in Sweden

4 the Rosens had to leave their homes or worry about being killed

LESSON 5 — Argue your opinion

Complete the chart below.

My opinion is . . .

I believe this because . . .

Another reason I think this is because . . .

You are now ready to argue your opinion!

LESSON 5

Give your opinion

What do you think about _____?

Write your opinion.

_____

_____

_____

_____

_____.

LESSON 6

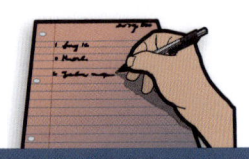

Write a new ending

If the soldiers below had heard the two families upstairs, what would have happened?

The soldiers would have _____

_____

_____

_____.

1 set the families free

2 taken the families to concentration camps

3 let the families live in their hiding place until after the war

LESSON 6 — Write character lines

Write out some lines based on the alternate ending you chose.

Choice 1: The soldiers would have set the families free and allowed them to go back to their homes.

Soldier: You are free to go back to your _____.

1. homes
2. cars
3. friends

Mr. Frank: Thank you so much. We are so happy to be _____

_____.

1. going to Sweden
2. going home
3. going away

LESSON 6 **Write character lines** (continued)

Write out some lines based on the alternate ending you chose.

Choice 2: The soldiers would have taken the families to concentration camps.

Soldier: You and your family, get down here right now! We are taking you to a _____.

1 church

2 sailboat

3 camp

Mr. Frank: Please, no! We want to go _____

_____.

1 to the camp

2 to our homes

3 to church

LESSON 6 **Write character lines** (continued)

Write out some lines based on the alternate ending you chose.

Choice 3: The soldiers would have allowed the families to keep hiding until the war was over.

Soldier: Get back in your homes and do not come out until _____

_____.

1 Christmas

2 the flood is over

3 the war is over

Mr. Frank: Thank you so much. We promise to be _____

_____.

1 very quiet

2 very loud

3 mean

LESSON 7 — **Write a poem**

Write your own poem. Try to include onomatopoeia.

_____

_____

_____

_____

_____

_____

Here are some ideas to write about:

- A time that you made a new friend
- A time that you felt that you were different
- A favorite game that you play
- Something unique about your neighborhood

LESSON 8 # KWHL

Fill in the KWHL chart.

Research Topic _____

KWHL Chart

What do you Know?	
What do you Want to know?	
How can you find out?	
What did you Learn?	

LESSON 8 KWHL

Fill in the KWHL chart.

Research Topic _____

KWHL Chart

What do you Know?	
What do you Want to know?	
How can you find out?	
What did you Learn?	

UNIT FOUR
Global Awareness

LESSON 1

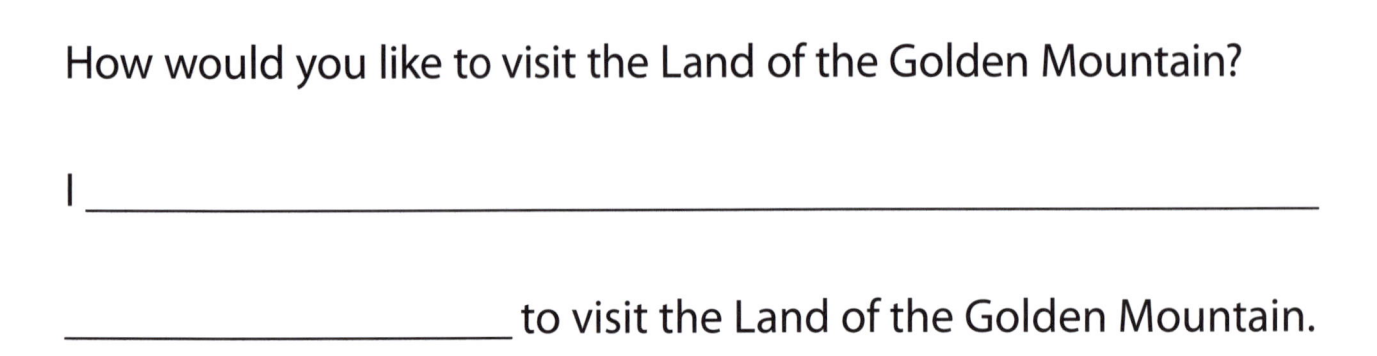

Give your opinion

How would you like to visit the Land of the Golden Mountain?

I _____

_____ to visit the Land of the Golden Mountain.

1 would like

2 would not like

LESSON 1 — **Support your opinion**

Support your opinion with a fact from the story.

I   **would like / would not like**   to visit the Land of the

Golden Mountain because _____

_____

_____.

1 the white demons might beat me up

2 I could make a lot of money

3 it's a dangerous place

4 I could look for gold at the mountain

LESSON 1

Critique your opinion

Do you still feel the same way, or have you changed your opinion? If you feel the same way, add another fact here to support your opinion. If you changed your mind, go to the next page.

☐ I have the same opinion.

I **would like / would not like** to visit the Land of the

Golden Mountain because _____

_____

and _____

_____.

1 the white demons might beat me up

2 I could make a lot of money

3 it's a dangerous place

4 I could look for gold at the mountain

LESSON 1

Critique your opinion (continued)

If you changed your mind, write a new opinion and support it with two facts.

☐ I changed my opinion.

Now I think I   **would like / would not like**   to visit the Land

of the Golden Mountain because _____

_____

and _____

_____.

1 the white demons might beat me up

2 I could make a lot of money

3 it's a dangerous place

4 I could look for gold at the mountain

DAILY WRITING JOURNAL • Unit Four

LESSON 1   **Argue your opinion**

Complete the chart below.

My opinion is . . .

I believe this because . . .

Another reason I think this is because . . .

You are now ready to argue your opinion!

LESSON 2 — Give your opinion

Who is your favorite character from Chapters 4 and 5?

My favorite character from Chapters 4 and 5 was _____

_____.

1 Uncle

2 Father

LESSON 2 — Support your opinion

Support your opinion with a fact from the story.

My favorite character from Chapters 4 and 5 was   **Uncle**   /

Father   because _____

_____

_____.

1 Uncle gave Father and Moon Shadow gifts

2 Uncle protected Father and Moon Shadow

3 Father beat up Black Dog

4 Father fixed the demon's horseless carriage

112 • DAILY WRITING JOURNAL • Unit Four

LESSON 2

Critique your opinion

Do you still feel the same way, or have you changed your opinion? If you feel the same way, add another fact here to support your opinion. If you changed your mind, go to the next page.

☐ I have the same opinion.

My favorite character from Chapters 4 and 5 was **Uncle** /

Father   because _____

_____

and _____

_____.

1 Uncle gave Father and Moon Shadow gifts

2 Uncle protected Father and Moon Shadow

3 Father beat up Black Dog

4 Father fixed the demon's horseless carriage

LESSON 2 **Critique your opinion** (continued)

If you changed your mind, write a new opinion and support it with two facts.

☐ I changed my opinion.

Now I think my favorite character from Chapters 4 and 5 was

Uncle / Father   because _____

_____

and _____

_____.

1 Uncle gave Father and Moon Shadow gifts

2 Uncle protected Father and Moon Shadow

3 Father beat up Black Dog

4 Father fixed the demon's horseless carriage

LESSON 2

Argue your opinion

Complete the chart below.

My opinion is . . .

I believe this because . . .

Another reason I think this is because . . .

You are now ready to argue your opinion!

LESSON 3

Give your opinion

Who is your favorite character from Chapters 6 and 7?

_____

_____ was my favorite character from Chapters 6 and 7.

1 Miss Whitlaw

2 Robin

LESSON 3 — **Support your opinion**

Support your opinion with a fact from the story.

Miss Whitlaw / **Robin**   was my favorite character from

Chapters 6 and 7 because _____

_____

_____.

1   she gave Moon Shadow milk and gingerbread cookies

2   she showed Moon Shadow Niagara Falls in a picture viewer

3   she had a friendly twinkle in her eye

4   she showed Moon Shadow the stained-glass window

DAILY WRITING JOURNAL • Unit Four

LESSON 3   # Critique your opinion

Do you still feel the same way, or have you changed your opinion? If you feel the same way, add another fact here to support your opinion. If you changed your mind, go to the next page.

☐ I have the same opinion.

I think **Miss Whitlaw / Robin** was my favorite character

from Chapters 6 and 7 because _____

_____

and _____

_____.

1 she gave Moon Shadow milk and gingerbread cookies

2 she showed Moon Shadow Niagara Falls in a picture viewer

3 she had a friendly twinkle in her eye

4 she showed Moon Shadow the stained glass window

LESSON 3 — **Critique your opinion** (continued)

If you changed your mind, write a new opinion and support it with two facts.

☐ I changed my opinion.

Now I think   **Miss Whitlaw / Robin**   was my favorite

character from Chapters 6 and 7 because _____

_____

and _____

_____.

1 she gave Moon Shadow milk and gingerbread cookies

2 she showed Moon Shadow Niagara Falls in a picture viewer

3 she had a friendly twinkle in her eye

4 she showed Moon Shadow the stained glass window

LESSON 3

Argue your opinion

Complete the chart below.

My opinion is . . .
_____
_____
I believe this because . . .
_____
_____
Another reason I think this is because . . .
_____
_____

You are now ready to argue your opinion!

LESSON 4

Describe an event

Describe what it might have been like to be in San Francisco after the earthquake.

1. There was a fire on Polk Street. I smelled _____

_____.

1 smoke

2 spaghetti

3 perfume

2. Some people were hurt. I heard someone yelling, _____

_____

1 "Happy birthday!"

2 "Help!"

3 "Timber!"

DAILY WRITING JOURNAL • Unit Four • 121

LESSON 4

Describe an event (continued)

3. As I looked around, I saw _____

_____

_____

_____.

1 rubble that had fallen down from buildings

2 children jumping rope

3 a lady quietly reading a book

LESSON 4

Give your opinion

There was an earthquake in the story. What do you think of the earthquake?

I think the earthquake was _____.

1 scary

2 sad

LESSON 4 — Support your opinion

Support your opinion with a fact from the story.

I think the earthquake was   **scary** / **sad**   because _____

_____

_____

_____.

1 people were crushed under the rubble

2 buildings were falling down

3 they heard no one calling—no one alive—after a while

4 life changed for everyone in San Francisco

LESSON 4 — **Critique your opinion**

Do you still feel the same way, or have you changed your opinion? If you feel the same way, add another fact here to support your opinion. If you changed your mind, go to the next page.

☐ I have the same opinion.

I think the earthquake was **scary / sad** because _____

_____

_____

and _____

_____.

1 people were crushed under the rubble

2 buildings were falling down

3 they heard no one calling—no one alive—after a while

4 life changed for everyone in San Francisco

LESSON 4 **Critique your opinion** (continued)

If you changed your mind, write a new opinion and support it with two facts.

☐ I changed my opinion.

Now I think the earthquake was   **scary / sad**   because _____

_____

_____

and _____

_____.

1 people were crushed under the rubble

2 buildings were falling down

3 they heard no one calling—no one alive—after a while

4 life changed for everyone in San Francisco

LESSON 4 — Argue your opinion

Complete the chart below.

My opinion is . . .

I believe this because . . .

Another reason I think this is because . . .

You are now ready to argue your opinion!

LESSON 5 — Give your opinion

Write your own opinion about the story.

My favorite part of the story was when _____

_____

_____

_____ .

1 Moon Shadow went to America

2 Father flew Dragonwings

3 Black Dog stole the money

4 Moon Shadow and his Mother and Father lived as a family

LESSON 5 — **Give your opinion**

How did you like this story?

I _____

_____ the story.

1 liked

2 did not like

DAILY WRITING JOURNAL • Unit Four

LESSON 5

Support your opinion

Support your opinion with a fact from the story.

I **liked** / **did not like** the story because _____

_____

_____

_____.

1 I thought it had a happy ending

2 Father crashed Dragonwings

3 Father and Moon Shadow moved away

4 Father fulfilled his dreams

LESSON 5 — **Critique your opinion**

Do you still feel the same way, or have you changed your opinion? If you feel the same way, add another fact here to support your opinion. If you changed your mind, go to the next page.

☐ I have the same opinion.

I **liked / did not like** the story because _____

_____

_____

and _____

_____.

1 I thought it had a happy ending

2 Father crashed Dragonwings

3 Father and Moon Shadow moved away

4 Father fulfilled his dreams

LESSON 5   **Critique your opinion** (continued)

If you changed your mind, write a new opinion and support it with two facts.

☐ I changed my opinion.

Now I   **like / do not like**   the story because _____

_____

_____

and _____

_____.

1   I think it had a happy ending

2   Father crashed Dragonwings

3   Father and Moon Shadow moved away

4   Father fulfilled his dreams

LESSON 5 — Argue your opinion

Complete the chart below.

My opinion is . . .

I believe this because . . .

Another reason I think this is because . . .

You are now ready to argue your opinion!

LESSON 5 **Describe an event**

Describe what it might have been like to be flying Dragonwings.

1. At the top of the hill, I could see all of San Francisco. It was so

_____.

1 smoky

2 beautiful

3 dark

2. I got ready to fly Dragonwings. I could hear my family and

friends yelling, _____

_____

1 "Good luck, Windrider!"

2 "You are crazy! Stop!"

3 "Be careful of the trees!"

LESSON 5

Describe an event (continued)

3. As Dragonwings started to fly, I felt _____

_____

_____.

1 afraid that Dragonwings would crash

2 this was just another boring day

3 proud that I had built an airplane

4. When Dragonwings crashed, I thought, _____

_____

1 "I made a mistake in flying it."

2 "I'm glad I tried."

3 "Ouch, that hurt."

LESSON 6 — Write a new ending

If Sadako had been able to fold a thousand paper cranes, what would have happened?

Sadako would have _____

_____

_____.

1 started running again

2 started feeling better again

3 moved back home

LESSON 6

Write character lines

Write out some lines based on the alternate ending you chose.

Choice 1: Sadako would have started running again.

Sadako: I feel so much better, I want to _____.

1 run

2 hike

3 ski

Chizuko: Great! If we train hard, you will be able to run in the

_____

_____.

1 big track meet

2 crane's pond

3 ski event

LESSON 6

Write character lines (continued)

Write out some lines based on the alternate ending you chose.

Choice 2: Sadako would have started feeling better again.

Doctor: You look like you are feeling much _____

_____.

1 better

2 happier

3 sadder

Sadako: I feel so much better! I think my _____

_____ has gone away.

1 rash

2 fever

3 leukemia

LESSON 6 — Write character lines (continued)

Write out some lines based on the alternate ending you chose.

Choice 3: Sadako would have moved back home.

Mrs. Sasaki: Welcome home Sadako. We _____

_____ you.

1 hate

2 missed

3 love

Sadako: I missed my family so much. It is good to be _____

_____.

1 home

2 at the hospital

3 running

LESSON 7

Write a poem

Write your own poem.

Title _____

Poem _____

_____

_____

_____

_____

_____

LESSON 7

Write a poem

Here are some ideas for a poem. Circle your choices to complete each line of the poem.

People

	CHOICE 1	CHOICE 2
Smiling _____.	faces	people
Bright _____.	eyes	expressions
We are all _____.	one	happy
Both girls and _____.	guys	boys
People are like _____.	shining stars	rainbows

LESSON 7
Write a poem

Here are some ideas for a poem. Circle your choices to complete each line of the poem.

I Can

	CHOICE 1	CHOICE 2
_____ can make a difference.	I	Everyone
We can all have _____.	peace	happiness
I will not _____.	fight	hate
I can be the _____	one	person
who changes _____.	the world	people

LESSON 8 KWHL

Fill in the KWHL chart.

Research Topic _____

KWHL Chart

What do you Know?	
What do you Want to know?	
How can you find out?	
What did you Learn?	

LESSON 8 KWHL

Fill in the KWHL chart.

Research Topic _____

KWHL Chart

What do you Know?	
What do you Want to know?	
How can you find out?	
What did you Learn?	